What Was It Like in Ancient China?

Logan Harrison

INFOMAX COMMON CORE READERS

Rosen Classroom™

New York

I0792494

Published in 2014 by The Rosen Publishing Group, Inc.
29 East 21st Street, New York, NY 10010

Book Design: Jon D'Rozario

Photo Credits: Cover feiyuezhangjie/Shutterstock.com; pp. 3, 4, 6, 7, 8, 9, 10, 12, 14, 16, 18, 20, 22, 23, 24 (bamboo) bonsay/Shutterstock.com; pp. 3, 4, 6, 7, 8, 9, 10, 12, 14, 16, 18, 20, 22, 23, 24 (texture) Nik Merkulov/Shutterstock.com; p. 5 (background) s_oleg/Shutterstock.com; p. 5 (map) Olinchuk/Shutterstock.com; p. 7 Jun Mu/Shutterstock.com; p. 9 szefei/Shutterstock.com; p. 11 TAO Images Limited/TAO Images/Getty Images; p. 13 testing/Shutterstock.com; p. 15 Stuart Jenner/Shutterstock.com; p. 17 beboy/Shutterstock.com; p. 19 Muellek Josef/Shutterstock.com; p. 21 (inset) Vivian Fung/Shutterstock.com; p. 21 (calligraphy) ariadna de raadt/Shutterstock.com p. 22 Pavel Vakhrushev/Shutterstock.com.

ISBN: 978-1-4777-2495-8
6-pack ISBN: 978-1-4777-2496-5

Manufactured in the United States of America

CPSIA Compliance Information: Batch #CS13RC: For further information contact Rosen Publishing, New York, New York at 1-800-237-9932.

Contents

A Land of Dynasties

China was home to some of the earliest civilizations (sih-vuh-luh-ZAY-shunz) on Earth. Civilizations are societies that form when people are settled and have advanced writing, art, science, and government. China is a large country with many mountains, but civilizations grew near its two main rivers: the Yangtze River and the Yellow River, or Huang He.

Time in ancient China was measured in dynasties. What's a dynasty? It's a period when all the rulers of an area come from the same family. The rulers in ancient China were called emperors.

The Yellow River and the Yangtze River were very important to life in ancient China and are still very important to Chinese people today!

Two Important Rivers

Yangtze River

3,915 miles (6,300 km) long

longest river in Asia

China's main waterway

other names: Long River, Great River

Yellow River

3,395 miles (5,464 km) long

second-longest river in China

known for its floods

other names: China's Sorrow, The Ungovernable, Mother River

The Shang Dynasty

Where does recorded history in China begin? It begins with the Shang Dynasty—the first dynasty to have written records. **Scholars** still don't agree on when the Shang Dynasty officially began. The date for the beginning of this dynasty is believed to be between 1760 and 1520 BC. The date for the end is believed to be between 1122 and 1030 BC.

Writings from the Shang Dynasty are found on oracle (OHR-uh-kuhl) bones. These are cow bones that **priests** used to answer people's questions about the future.

Chinese priests would make and read cracks on oracle bones in order to tell people what their future would be.

Ancient Chinese Families

Oracle bones show the Shang Dynasty's history as well as family names from that period. The family was the most important part of life in ancient China.

The father was the family leader. Women were seen as less important than men. Their fathers ruled their lives until they married. Then, they were ruled by their husbands. A woman whose husband had died was ruled by her oldest son. Boys could go to school, but girls couldn't.

Family is still a very important part of life in China.

Home Sweet Home

There was a big difference between rich people and poor people in ancient China. Rich people lived in very large homes. These were usually made out of wood with tiles on the roof. These homes had very beautiful gardens. The entire house was built around a courtyard.

Poor people in ancient China lived in much smaller homes. These homes often had roofs made of plant **material**. In both big and small homes, families prayed at **shrines** to their **ancestors**.

You can still see shrines in Chinese homes today.

子孫繁衍耀宗功

The Power of Heaven

People in ancient China believed their ancestors would help them in times of need. They also believed in many gods. However, ancient Chinese people believed that one god, Heaven, had more power than the rest. They believed Heaven had the power to choose the emperor! This power was known as the Mandate of Heaven.

When bad things happened in China, such as floods or **droughts**, it was believed that the emperor had lost the Mandate of Heaven. A new emperor was then chosen.

The Temple of Heaven was built to honor Heaven. It's a popular place to visit in China!

Two Classes

In ancient China, there were two social classes that people fell into: the upper class and the lower class. The emperor was at the top of society. Who else made up the upper class? Government workers who had to pass special tests were in the upper class. Scholars and businesspeople who owned land were also part of this class.

Who made up ancient China's lower class? Soldiers, scientists, and merchants were in this class. The poorest people were at the bottom of society.

Scientists are respected in China today, but in ancient times they were in the lower class of society.

Farmers in ancient China were often poor and in the lower class. They often grew grains, such as wheat and rice. Tea and cotton were also grown on ancient Chinese farms. Farmers raised animals, too. Chickens and pigs were common farm animals in ancient China.

People also caught fish for food in China's many rivers. Rich people ate this fish, along with many other meats, grains, and vegetables. Poor people in ancient China could often afford to eat only rice or noodles made from wheat.

Farmers have grown rice in China for thousands of years. They still grow it today.

How Did They Travel?

How did farmers get their grain to cities in ancient China? They used canals, which are man-made waterways built to carry goods. Ancient China also had many roads for traveling over land. By 210 BC, there were over 4,000 miles (6,436 km) of roads throughout China!

The ancient Chinese people also built bridges. They were good at building bridges strong enough to last for many years. Some of the bridges built in ancient China continue to be used over 1,000 years later!

How long will ancient Chinese bridges last?
People may still use them many years from now.

Ancient Chinese Art

Art was an important part of life in ancient China. During the Shang Dynasty, people began using bronze—a yellow-brown metal—to make useful things, such as bowls, as well as art. Jade, a green stone, was also a popular material for making art in ancient China.

One of the most famous ancient Chinese arts was calligraphy (kuh-LIH-gruh-fee), which means "beautiful writing." People used ink, a brush, and paper to make special art with Chinese characters. Boys learned calligraphy in school.

Which of these kinds of ancient Chinese art would you want to learn to make?

How Is It Different?

Life in ancient China might seem very different from our lives today, but we still use many things that were invented during that time. Do you like to watch fireworks? The ancient Chinese invented fireworks using gunpowder. They were also the first people to write on a kind of paper. Silk, a material still found in our clothes, was first made and used in ancient China.

How is your life different from life in ancient China? Are there any things that are the same?

Glossary

ancestor (AN-sehs-tuhr) Someone in your family who lived long before you.

drought (DROWT) A long period of dry weather.

material (muh-TIHR-ee-uhl) Something from which something else can be made.

priest (PREEST) A person who leads or performs religious activities.

scholar (SKAH-luhr) A person who has done advanced studying.

shrine (SHRYN) A place to honor a god or ancestor.

Index